# A Pocket Guide To Starting A Podcast

Nate E. Butkus

ISBN: 9068525
ISBN-13: 978-1726255394

# DEDICATION

To  Mrs. Retzinger, my favorite teacher and an inspiration
to everyone she teaches.

# CONTENTS

# INTRODUCTION

So why a pocket guide? I wanted this resource to be a little bit quick and easy to use. So if you ever want to start a podcast, you can pull this book out, read through it and start a podcast.

By the way, my name is Nate Butkus. I host a podcast called The Show About Science which started when I was 5 years old. The Show About Science is a podcast for kids and adults. For kids, it helps their minds grow with facts, while also being kind of funny. I interview scientists and other experts to learn more about topics I love. For me, podcasting changed the way I saw the world for the better. I realized that on my show, I could give amazing breakthroughs and dangerous topics the attention they deserved. But most importantly, podcasting is fun – especially getting to meet and interview all sorts of really interesting people and then sharing the details of what I learn with my listeners.

Now I'm 8 years old and on a mission to share what I've learned. And the biggest thing I've learned is that people can do anything they want as long as they put their mind to it and don't let anything stand in their way. And hopefully this book will be the guide you need to get started!

# 1. NAME YOUR PODCAST

So the first thing you need to do is decide what your podcast is about and name it, but don't think too hard about it. Naming can be easy as long as you don't think too deep and second guess it. Make sure you choose a good name because that is what your name will be forever.

The way to tell if it's a good name is if it comes from your heart and you've thought it through and you've decided that you're willing to go with it.

The way to tell if it's a bad name is if you just thought of it and decided "hey this would be a good name." But then later, you think "I really should change this." Trust your instincts.

# 2. DEFINE WHAT YOUR SHOW/EPISODE IS ABOUT

When defining your podcast, the name will play an important role. Choosing a broad topic will allow for many episodes. For example, a show about science is broader than a show about astronomy. A show like Reply All is very broad. They bill themselves as a show about the internet. Which makes it easier to come up with episode ideas.

You need to figure out topics that come from your heart. It's basically as easy as talking about your favorite things. And if you want, you can have guests, but you don't have to have guests. You can have a storytelling show, a show with multiple hosts, a music show or you can just talk about your favorite topic, but this pocket guide will be focusing on shows with guests.

# 3. WHO TO INTERVIEW

So how do you pick who to interview? Well, look on the internet and find people who match the premise of the topic your podcast is all about. Another way to find good guests is to think, "do I know anyone who would be good to interview in this field?" You can also read articles or watch documentaries and see who was interviewed or who contributed. Good guests will always be excited to answer your questions and know a lot about the topic.

# 4. DO YOUR RESEARCH

What are the best ways to do your research? Watching videos on YouTube is the easiest way to do research, especially if you're a 5 year old who can't read like I was when I started my show. The best videos are the short videos that you learn a lot from. Videos tell you about some things, but not in detail, so you can still learn a lot from your guest. That makes the interview more fun.

Besides videos, there are also books, newspapers, magazines, documentaries and scientific journals. You can even listen to other podcasts to conduct your research.

Always have fun while doing your research, but remember, the most important thing to remember is the better job you do with your research, the better your interview will be.

# 5. THINK OF QUESTIONS

The questions you ask your guests are very important. You can come up with questions ahead of time, but you can also come up with them on the spot as long as you've done your research and understand the topic. Thinking of questions in advance will mean you don't need to be worried about what your next question will be. They're a good way to get a more polished sounding episode.

But, if you want a more casual sounding episode just think of questions right then and there by building off what your guest is saying. Listen to what your guest is saying so you can have a conversation. You have no idea how much this will help you. The interview sounds so much better when you listen!

# 6. CONDUCT THE INTERVIEW

When conducting your interview, you should always be a good host and make your guest feel welcome. Be chatty and have a conversation. It will make your listeners much more engaged. Asking good questions is the key to being a good interviewer. A question is good if it's something you can relate to, and the audience can relate to, and it gets a really interesting answer out of the guest. Avoid any questions that have "yes" or "no" answers because they don't move you along at all in the episode. Keep your guest talking!

# 7. EDIT THE INTERVIEW

Editing the interview is a very important step to eliminating all the jagged audio edges in your work. It is one of the last steps too! Editing is a very long step, but you must do it if you want to make your podcast good and popular. You have to listen back to your work, put things into what works and what doesn't, cut out all the things that don't work, and keep what does for your episode. You can also move questions around and change the order of them to make the episode roll along smoother. In order to reach audio perfection, you must edit.

# 8. ADD VOICEOVER, MUSIC AND SOUND EFFECTS

Capping off the editing part of an episode, you'll begin adding final touches to your amazing podcast with voiceover, music and sound effects! Add in new strips of audio to make your work sound complete like an introduction, conclusion and transitions.   This step will make your podcast sound phenomenal and ready to be listened to. With this step done, you will be ready to publish your episode!

# 9. PUBLISH YOUR EPISODE

Time to publish your episode! There are lots of places where you can do this like iTunes and SoundCloud. Great, now your podcast is out there! This is the most important step in podcasting since no one will be able to listen to your podcast if you do not follow this step. Period. Ok still with me? Great! Now you have a real podcast with one more thing to go! Time to find out what it is…

# 10. PROMOTE YOUR EPISODE

Ok, the last step is to promote your episode. You can go crazy with this one. Posters, books, inventions, and car stickers can help you get more listeners. A social media presence on sites like Twitter, Facebook or Instagram can also help you promote your podcast, connect with your listeners and have a head start in podcasting. In the end, you will have created a well-crafted work of art. Now it's time to get started on episode two!

Nate E. Butkus

# HELPFUL WEBSITES

This chapter is for those of you who might need a little help finding music, sound effects and listeners. This is my list of helpful websites:

- Sounds Like An Earful
- SoundCloud
- Kids Listen
- Apple Podcasts
- Anchor.fm
- Threadless

# EQUIPMENT

## Studio Equipment:
- Electrovoice RE20 microphone
- Google Voice for Phone Interviews
- Adobe Audition
- Facetime
- Zencaster
- Audio Interface (RME, Focusrite or Tascam)

## On Location Equipment:
- Audiotechnica 8035 microphone
- TASCAM DR40 audio recorder
- Sennheiser wireless microphone

# NOTES:

# NOTES:

# NOTES:

# NOTES:

# ABOUT THE AUTHOR

Nate Butkus is the 8 year old host of his own podcast, *The Show About Science*. He is also a photographer and a good one too! He is also a figure skater, although not Olympic level. He wrote this book to teach others how to podcast.

www.ingramcontent.com/pod-product-compliance
Lightning Source LLC
Chambersburg PA
CBHW071554080326
40690CB00056B/2045